Clearing with Purpose
A Psychic's Story
Goo & Cookies Book

Auriel Grace
ISBN: 9781728792637
Copy Write 11/6/2018

I dedicate this book to my 'Ohana – my Family –

Vicki 'Star' Harding, Mom, Jessica Ia, Sandy Kusy (AKA TigerLady), My Bro THEO, Cindy 'LiteHope' Moss, Rockin Reverend Rhonda and Mike Schienle, Bambi Harris, Molly Jones, Katie Girl, Ella Bo Bella, Gunnar, Anissa and Mark Chmura, Melinda Carver, Kris & Pauli Sedersten, Kat Hobson, Hanna – Sunshine Girl – O'Dell, Darla Tegtmeier, Susan and Tracy 'Batman' Todd, Lisa V. So many more!

Table of Content

In the moment of my soul's conception the Creators in their wisdom endowed my soul with great gifts and gave me the power of choice . . . Auriel Grace

What to Expect

In this day and age, you have forgotten you were created from love, joy, wonder . . . This is at the core of your being. Humans have created a hard core of duality around themselves. It is time now to shed your shell and get to your core! The Archeia Divine compliments of the Arch Angels.

This is my favorite part of working with people. I love assisting with clearing out all energy that does not serve in their lives. I call it releasing goo and cooties. This book is going to give you some ideas, tools to help you release energy, emotions, thoughts and perhaps relationships no longer serving you. Let's go deep and clear out what is not working for you and bring to the surface of what works for you!

The subjects covered in this book will help you with your Clair's – clairvoyance, clairaudience, clairsentience, claircognizance and more. You will have the tools you need to help yourself, family and friends.

There are techniques in this book I have been using for years, clearing out my Goo & Cooties. I have written them so you can make them your own. As with anything you do it takes practice. Remember to be patient and loving with yourself as you clear out your own Goo and Cooties.

I have placed a glossary at the end of this book for you to refer too to help you out. If you are working on your intuitive skills in any area of your life this is a great place to start with clearing your body, mind and spirit.

I suggest you read I am Psychic, not Telepathic before reading this book, there is information in that book that will help you with this one. You know there is going to be homework, that will be very fun for you.

Are you ready? Let's flex those intuitive muscles!

The Power of Sound

Every sound has power. Why? Sound is Energy.

Have you ever been to a gong Meditation? The sound is so spectacular, it just rolls all around you and clears your energy field all the way down to your physical body. Maybe you have had a toning session, those tones just rock you into the cosmos, right? Powerful!

How about music, different kinds of music help us feel different ways, right? Powerful those sounds.

Each living being puts out a certain frequency as well, we are powerful beings just being. Our thoughts, words and deeds have energy and are the driving force in our lives. What kind of sounds are you making?

This is why it is important to clear out old hurts. When you speak on the subject, you voice will reflect that emotion. That reflection goes out into your energy field and hangs out there with you until you clear it out. Every time you release an old hurt you raise your resonance, is that cool or what?

Pay attention to how you communicate and how others communicate with you. Remember a good communicator is also a good listener. Listen to inflection, pitch, accent and how the people use their words. Do they edit or hold back their words? Do you?

You may have to change the way you communicate so you can be heard the way you want to be. Consider the vibes you are putting out there. That's what you are getting back. If you are unhappy, pay attention to how you communicate with others. It's ok, to look at it and make the shift. I certainly have had to do this myself and it does take practice and perseverance.

Start with Intention. In I am Psychic, not Telepathic, we practiced creating Intentions and being grateful. Write down what you are grateful for, add to the list. This will raise your resonance, which will also change the way you communicate. Write down your intentions, what do you truly want to create. This will also shift you into a higher vibration and help you focus on how you want your life.

Intention is powerful, why? Because when you focus and you make a decision, that goal becomes a vibration, a sound and it can be heard across the cosmos.

I intend my heart is open and aligned with the energy of love.

This is an intention that reminds me to connect and open up. I have said it so many times now, all I have to do is feel the resonance of it and I come back into alignment with my true self.

You will learn how to invoke your spirit guides, angels, ascended masters and more for some of your assignments. You will see or feel how powerful you are through these clearing sessions or ceremonies. Some of you will want to create a ceremony around what you learn here and that is awesome. Just remember, as you create, you make sound, be clear while you create.

What is an invocation? An Invocation is a call or an invitation. It is a prayer and intention. That is how we will be using invocations through the different clearing practices in this book. For example, before I start working on this book I always Invite and invoke Lord Melchizedek, Lady Nada and Archeia Grace to assist with my writing so you get what is for your highest and greatest good. This is what it looks like –

I invite and invoke Lord Melchizedek, Lady Nada and Archeia Grace for the perfect words for this project's highest and greatest good. Thank you!

When I say the invocation, I mean it. I connect to my Solar Plexus and my Heart Chakra and pull energy from those areas to put energy in those words.

Create and invocation, say it out loud. Did the area around you shift? What does it feel like? How do you feel?

Homework –

Observe how you communicate with others. How do others communicate with you?

How can you make changes in the way your words affect others?

Write and say what you are grateful for.

Write and say your intentions.

Notes:

Aloha & 'Ohana

When people ask me my opinion of paradise, I always tell them, North Shore, Oahu, Hawaii. It is the most beautiful beach I have ever visited, played at and surfed. I love Hawaii, you can walk down the street, pick fruit and eat it in the neighborhood, grow gardens all year round. I love the smell of plumeria flowers in the morning. The people of Hawaii are most welcoming and loving, besides it being absolutely beautiful.

Hawaii helped me create the awesome career I have now. The local people of Hawaii are wonderful and supportive. It truly is a place of love energy. I lived in Hawaii during a time of prosperity for local artists. My jewelry making business did great, I started my career of doing intuitive readings during this time as well. I gave birth to both my sons on the island of Oahu, in Manoa Valley at Kapiolani hospital.

While living in Hawaii, I had my first concept of what a soul group is. While living there, I made good friends, friends I will always remember and cherish. They taught me about 'Ohana – family. We have our blood family ties, which helps us develop our structure and foundation. Our blood family teaches us a lot about discernment, respect and love.

Our 'Ohana, is our blood family, friends and community and the deep connection we have to it. In Hawaii if a child or person calls you auntie, uncle, grandma or grandpa it is a sign of respect. You are their 'Ohana, family and community.

Our 'Ohana in my opinion is our soul group and our deep connection to each individual soulmate, we have more than one soulmate. Soulmates are not just our lovers or mates. They are our petty tyrants, hardest people on us, our friends, siblings, parents and more. Our soul group is always there to help us with our hardest lessons and to show us how wondrous our lives can be if we allow them and how wondrous we are.

Do you feel deep connections to people who are in your life or those who have passed through your life?

There is always a gain through relationship, what did you gain from your soul group or soulmates?

The other concept I learned about was Aloha. Many tourists think Aloha means hello and goodbye because when you get off the plane you are greeted with someone saying Aloha to you. Aloha means love, compassion and mercy. What a beautiful greeting and intention to people visiting the islands. We can all use love, compassion and mercy. Think about Aloha while you are reading this book and doing the work you will be doing.

Aloha and Mahalo!

Home work –

Who do you consider your soul group or 'Ohana is and why?

Notes:

Soul Groups & Soul Mates

A Soul group is a group that travels together through all space and time. The soul group is constantly learning through relationships created within the group. When you pay attention to your life you will see those who are part pf your soul group. You will feel the recognition deep within your being, pay attention, be present.

Look around at those people who surround you now. How do you feel about them?

Think of all the events that stand out in your heart and memory, perhaps you met someone in passing and felt déjà vu or a connection when you saw them. What was the end result of that meeting?

Those who are part of your soul group are your soulmates. Some of those soul mates you might think you have a deep connection with because you do not agree or have a dislike for that person(s). Look closely at the relationship and pay attention to the development of it. There is a lesson or a balance of karma happening. It is up to you to take a breath, connect and figure out what you agreed to do. It may be something so simple as no reaction or acknowledgement, to love them as they are.

Many people think of soul mates in a romantic way. There are romantic soul mate relationships that last the lifetime and what a blessing it is to be part of an opportunity such as that. Truly look deeply at your mate, forgive what needs to be forgiven, see and appreciate them for who they are. You may realize this person is your soulmate and the relationship is what you make of it. So, if you need more of something in the relationship then communicate that to your mate.

I want to point out there is no one outside of yourself that can complete you. You are the only person who can acknowledge that. Be wondrous, be you!

Here is a fun example of one of my soul mates –

I have a friend I call Mr. Bill. Yes, his name is Bill. I met him in Virginia. He was working on a project for the pyramids in the Giza Plateau in Egypt. He walked into my store on day and exclaimed – Mary, I have been looking for you! (He calls me Mary, past life reference).

I didn't freak out when he said he had been looking for me. My soul about leaped out of my body as I watched Mr. Bill walk toward me smiling. I knew him and I was glad to see him too. We fell back into friendship, and it was very nice to see him again. We worked on some projects together which was fun. When we were done with our projects, we parted in Virginia, I went to the Four Corners Region and he went to Northern Virginia. We kept in touch as the years went by. One day I got an email from him asking me if I knew where Pagosa Springs Colorado was. I was living there and I emailed him back and let him know what my phone number was. He called me five minutes later. He just moved about a mile away from my house with his new wife. I went to see him that afternoon, it was so nice to see him again and be able to spend time with him. We worked together on some more project and he left for Egypt.

I haven't heard from Mr. Bill in a while, sometimes I feel his energy moving around the planet and its very nice I was able to connect with him in this lifetime.

I have had several friendships like that. We come together to work on project and when we are done we move on, know we will see each other again in this life or the next and its okay.

My big lesson in this lifetime is setting boundaries and enforcing them. My soul group has shown up for my lesson in a big way and I am grateful to all of them for their assistance, even if I didn't like it when it was happening.

Homework –

Can recognize your soulmates?

How do each of them feel to you? Remembering your soulmates are there to assist you through your life lessons.

Have you experienced Déjà vu when meeting someone? How did you feel?

Notes:

Chakras

Chakras – The 7 energy centers of the body. Each chakra has its own purpose, color and is 2/3 inches in diameter. The chakra is a spinning vortex tube reaching through the front of your body to your back.

The Chakra looks like a beautifully, flowing, spinning vortex. All Chakras are about 2/3 inches in diameter and spinning at a comfortable speed. They are our energy centers, they effect different areas of our bodies depending on how stimulated the vortices are.

Root/Base Chakra – This chakra is red. This is your foundations and the need to survive. It is the seat of the **Kundalini** energy. This Chakra is also about you being present, trusting, grounded, stable and secure in your life.
Under active – fearful nervous, unwelcoming
Overactive – materialistic/greedy, obsessed w/ being secure, resistant to change
The Root Chakra is located at the base of the spine.
Scents – Patchouli, Vetivert, Thyme,
Stones – Black Agate, Red Jasper,
Tone – C

Spleen/ Sacral Chakra – This Chakra is Orange. This is your creative center. This is the center where you create life and where the energy comes to create in the living world. When this chakra is open, your feelings flow freely and you are expressive. Open to intimacy, passionate and lively.

Under active – unemotional, not open

Over active – Emotional, attachment to people, overly sexual

Scents – Sandalwood, Cardamom, Clary Sage

Stone – Carnelian

Tone - D

This chakra is located one inch below the belly button.

Will/ Solar Plexus Chakra – This Chakra is Yellow. This is where the energy for Clairsentience and self-esteem comes from. The Will to create your life!

Under active – passive, indecisive, timid, feel like you never get what you want.

Overactive - domineering/aggressive

Scents – Juniper, Hyssop, Lime, Marjoram

Stone – Citrine

Tone - E

This Chakra is located three inches above the belly button.

Heart Chakra – this chakra is Emerald Green or Pink. This is the Mediating center of the Chakras – Center for higher love and healing energies. You will feel comfortable with love, kindness, affection, compassionate, friendly, harmonious.

Under active – cold and distant

Over active – suffocating people with love, selfish

reasons for love
Scents – geranium, bergamot, ylang ylang, jasmine, lavender
Stones – Rose Quartz/ Aventurine
Tone - F
The heart chakra is located three inches above the Solar plexus.

Throat Chakra – This chakra is Turquoise. This is the communication center and the center for telepathy, hearing and clairaudience. You will feel comfortable with self-expression and creativity.
Under active – introverted, shy, not speaking your truth
Over active – talk too much, keep people at a distance, bad listener
Scents – Chamomile, Basil, peppermint, rosemary
Stone – Turquoise,
Tone - G
The throat chakra is located in the throat area.

Brow or 3rd Eye Chakra – This chakra is Indigo – Clairvoyance or higher and clearer perceptions – spiritual vision.
You will be comfortable with insight, visualization, you have good intuition, fantasize
Under active – not good at thinking for the self. Rigid in thinking, relying on beliefs too much. Confused easily
Over active – fantasizing too much, hallucinations
Scents – Lemon, Pine, Hyacinth

Stones – Iolite, Amethyst
Tone - A
The third eye chakra is located in the center of the forehead.

Crown – Violet or white – aligns us with the higher forces of the Universe and our direct connection to our Divine
Source. You are comfortable with higher wisdom and with being one in the world. Unprejudiced.
Under active – Not spiritually aware, rigid in your thinking.
Overactive – Intellectualizing too much, addicted to spirituality and ignoring bodily needs.
Scents – Neroli, Myrrh, Rose
Stones – Amethyst or Quartz
Tone - B
The Crown Chakra is located at the crown of the head.

Keeping our chakras balance and in alignment is really important while we are clearing. We want to make sure our chakras are sparkling, happily and they spin. One way you can do this is by doing the Chakra Meditation on my website once a month for maintenance.

Look at the information written above on the under active or over active areas of each chakra. What are your imbalances? There is different idea in each chakra to assist with balancing out. For a long time, I did not feel 'safe'. This imbalance was in my root chakra. I had to do a lot of work to clear the feeling of not being 'safe' in this lifetime. Part of this feeling came from other lifetimes of being a spiritual person rather than a religious person. Once I realized this I was able to clear out the fear and adjust to this lifetime. I realized also it doesn't really matter what others think of me as long as I happy and content in my life. I am that very much so, now that I took the steps to clear out the old fear.

Once I strengthened my root chakras, my others chakras brightened and strengthened as well. I could feel my physical body start to unwind as I worked with this chakra to bring it back into balance. My emotional reaction to people wanting to convert me or tell me I was 'crazy' for my practices. Now I just smile and wave at them. No reaction, they are people to with their own journey.

Another way of maintaining our chakras is cutting the golden cords. What are the golden cords? They are cords from other people we know. If you have a lot of cording you might be experiencing aches and pain in or around your chakras.

To see your cords, take a breath and focus on your chakras, you will feel/see them. They are golden, older cords look antique gold. Some of the cords will be thick some of them will be thin, like string. Don't freak out when you see how many you have. You are going to get some tools to use to cut cords. Remember to do the Chakra meditation. That will help you.

I always have a cord cutting ceremony done for me every time my life changes. This helps me move forward without having to repeat a lesson and for maintenance and clarity on all levels. When you are looking for a practitioner who does these ceremonies make sure they invoke Arch Angel Michael for the ceremony. This ceremony is very powerful. You will feel great afterward. There may be some grief, that's okay, let it go, you are moving forward.

For daily maintenance for clearing out cording I say this invocation –

I invite and invoke Arch Angel Michael to cut and cauterize all energetic cords leading in and out of me for my highest and greatest good. I invite and invoke Archeia Faith to fill me with Divine Light to heal all of my hurts and wounds. Thank you!

Then I spin a vortex –

Take a breath and quiet your mind.
Visualize a vortex or tornado circling your feet.
With each breath you take, the vortex rises over your body sinning faster and faster.

As the vortex spins you allow it to pull out of your field all those thoughts and energies that no longer serve you.

Visualize the vortex move up over your legs, hips, core, neck and head until you hear a pop. Your energetic field is now clear!

Keeping your energy field and chakras balanced and clear help on all levels and space and time. You will feel more energy flow through you and out of you. It helps sharpen your intuition and instinct and raises your resonance.

There are also Heart strings. They Heart strings are located in in your Heart chakra. Those are also golden strings and go from you to your love ones. You can strengthen your heart strings by focusing on them and moving love energy through them to your love ones to strengthen the bond between you and them. Keep your love and Heart Chakra healthy by doing this whenever you feel like you want to connect to your loved ones.

Homework – Practice daily –

I invite and invoke Arch Angel Michael to cut and cauterize all energetic cords leading in and out of me for my highest and greatest good. I invite and invoke Archeia Faith to fill me with Divine Light to heal all of my hurts and wounds. Thank you!

Spin a vortex –

Take a breath and quiet your mind.
Visualize a vortex or tornado circling your feet.
With each breath you take, the vortex rises over your body sinning faster and faster.

As the vortex spins you allow it to pull out of your field all those thoughts and energies that no longer serve you.

Visualize the vortex move up over your legs, hips, core, neck and head until you hear a pop. Your energetic field is now clear!

Notes:

Energy

The shifting of energy is very subtle most of the time. This is why it is very important to be present in your life, being aware of what is going on around you to feel the shifts in energy.

What is in your Energy Field or Aura?

You carry with you, different energies in your aura or energy field, here is a list of examples you may carry with you -

Love	Fear
Success	Sadness/Sorrow
Compassion	Anger/Frustration
Courage	Abandonment
Hope	Despair
Faith	Insecurity

The list can go on, those are examples above.

How do you clear out those ideas, emotions that no longer serve you?

We will use Sadness/Sorrow for our example- (Many time we don't even know where so much of this sadness and sorrow comes from)

In most of the clients I work with the sadness/sorrow comes from other lifetimes as well as this lifetime. It is in your energy field, although you may not feel it all the time the energy is heavily in your aura or energy field. When energy such as this stays in the aura or energy field it draws people and situations of sorrow and sadness to you.

There are many ways you can help yourself out with clearing your energy field. Energy work such as Reiki, Cord Cutting Ceremonies, Cranial Sacral, Soul Retrieval, meditation - these types of healing processes can assist you with clearing your energy field of anything that does not serve you.

Observe others, tune into facial expressions and body movements with people. While having a conversation with your friend or family member, observe and listen. What are you hearing and seeing outside of what is being said? Can you feel or see shifts in energy around or within the person outside of what is being said?

Observe and tune into your environment(s), be present, you will feel the subtle energies around you and you will know how or when to interact with the people seen and unseen in these places. When I walk into a place whether I have been there or not, I always pause and look around with my eyes, and other senses, so I know what I am walking into.

Energy vampires are those people who push for you to react to what they are saying or doing to tap into your energy and drain you. Some of these people know what they are doing, some are totally clueless.

Those who do know what they are doing are very subtle in their manipulations. They are predators. They will work to manipulate you into reacting to them so you have a burst of energy. They suck your energy up like a martini and you are exhausted from the interaction. How do you keep them from doing this?

Create a bubble around you including under your feet, mirrors facing outward, make the bubble nice and thick. You want those mirrors facing outward so no one can energetically cord into you. Make it a habit every day before you leave your home to protect yourself like this. Your energy is yours, no one else's.

Now that you know the person is an energetic vampire you can ask them calmly to find another way to get your attention. I used to do this when my kids tried to throw a fit or be bad. When someone would call me, and complain about their life and family.

'Find another way of getting my attention.'

When you say this to the person, they will be caught off balance and when they are centered again they will try again. Remind them to find a different way of getting your attention and give them examples of acceptable ways of getting your attention.

'If you have nothing nice to say, don't say anything,"

This will knock an energy vampire of balance too. They will try to get a reaction out of you from this. Be calm, firm and loving. Give them a hug and explain to them this sort of behavior is no longer acceptable. Let them know they are loved, be firm with this new boundary you have set up with them. This is you respecting your space, how awesome is that?

Here is an example –

I had a client who was attracted to me. We met weekly for soul retrieval and clearing work. One night he saw me at the hot springs, we had a nice conversation and I left.

He subconsciously sent a cord out into my second chakra. The next day I was on my back with my daughter Christa looking over me, she did her best to assist me in pulling the cord out. We couldn't get it out and I was in a lot of pain. Christa went to talk to him. She walked him through removing the cord. I was able to breathe energy into the injured chakra to heal it. It took three days for the pain in my lower back to heal. After that, I made sure my protective bubble was really thick and mirrored so no one could cord into me like that again.

This is not an appropriate way of telling someone you are attracted to them. If you are attracted to someone let them know. It is good to express feelings. If you cannot find the words, wait until you can and then express yourself. If you feel it is inappropriate for you to tell the person, write a letter and do not send it. Then your feelings have been expressed and you are relieved of the intense feelings. Do not wait until your feelings are leaking out of you. This is not healthy and you want to be healthy on all levels.

Everyone has cords from many different relationships. There is nothing wrong with this. What you need to pay attention too is why you have those cords and what you can do to release these cords.

Go Vertical!

Being centered, grounded and connected to your higher self and Divine Source is really important. Why? Well when you are practicing this you make clear decisions, and you will feel confident in your decisions. You will be aware of what's going on in your environment, at home, work or at play.

Going Vertical helps you be aware of the people you inner act with and how they inner act with you. It also helps you protect yourself against anyone who would attack you psychically and how you can deflect it.

Children know internally what 'Go Vertical' means. When my youngest son was in the second grade he was in a rowdy classroom room. He used to tell his classmates to 'Go Vertical' so much his teacher asked me what it meant. I explained to her, that is what I told my children when they got out of hand and it would help them come back to center. She understood and started herself using the term for the class. It worked, the second graders would simmer down so she could do her job.

Try it with your family and see what happens!

Homework –
Practice thickening up your bubble before you leave the house every day. How do you feel? Be aware of the people around you, how do you feel around them.

Spin a Vortex daily

Take a breath and quiet your mind.
Visualize a vortex or tornado circling your feet.
With each breath you take, the vortex rises over your body sinning faster and faster.

As the vortex spins you allow it to pull out of your field all those thoughts and energies that no longer serve you.

Visualize the vortex move up over your legs, hips, core, neck and head until you hear a pop. Your energetic field is now clear!

Cut the Golden Cords daily
Invocation - I invite & Invoke Arch Angel Michael to cut and Cauterize all cords leading in and out of me that no longer serve me, I invite and invoke Archeia Faith to fill me with Divine Light to heal all my wounds and hurts!

Notes:

Karma

Karma, what is it?

There are three types of Karma –
Sanchita Karma – the sum total of past karma yet to be resolved.
Prarabdha Karma – the sum of Sanchita Karma to be experienced in this life.
Kriyamana Karma – the Karma humans are creating will bear fruit in the future.

Karma is a constant energy. Every time you do a deed whether you consider it good or bad you create Karma. Karma is often confused with soul contracts we created in the beginning of each life time. Soul Contracts and Karma go hand in hand, together, always.

Karma is not revenge, it's energy we manifest through our thoughts, words and deeds.

Before we come into each lifetime we decide what and how we want to learn, grow and who we wanted to learn with. We create what we want to learn, release and experience before coming into each life. We decide what is best for our soul's growth.

Before we go further, think about your life and the experiences in it, create a timeline, starting with the first thing you remember and start there. You can break down your timelines and get creative with them. Look at the events that have brought you to the place you are now.

What have you learned?
How have you grown?

It took me three years to write my timelines. I wanted to break down events felt were creating emotional blocks in my life. I stopped at places in my timeline to think about the events and clear out any energy that was holding me in place. My goal was emotional freedom at the time. I wanted to be free of any emotional energy that was blocking my forward movement.

When I got to a place in my timeline that was embarrassing or painful, I would connect to it to release the emotion, the event or the person. Then I said – with reference to me.

I love you
I bless you
I thank you
I forgive you
I release you

When you do this, you push the energy out of you and your energy field. You are releasing. It may take several times to do this. Be patient and compassionate with yourself as you do your release work. Let it go willingly and completely. When you do this, you make room for all the wondrousness you want to bring into your life. Be Courageous, be a Warrior!

For some of the painful events in my life it took time for me to truly to release the energy. Be patient with yourself, love yourself and be thankful for your life, it is the only life you will have being the person you are now. Do not let goo and cooties hold you back from a wondrous and joyous life.

I learned a lot about myself and others while writing my timelines, I was able to forgive or start forgiving people and events in my life. It was really a relief for me when I started doing this for myself and I saw that through this experience I was able to move forward with my life with more ease and grace.

One of the ideas I discovered about myself is I love the concept of freedom on all levels in all time and space. I always felt uncomfortable with the idea of being dependent. As I delved into past lives and this life I saw times where I was forced to be dependent on people. Now in this lifetime, I am a woman, a single mother, I had to learn about independence and how awesome it is.

What a great idea it was for me to be born in America, a woman and single mother to figure that out. I cherish my freedom to create as I please. This is a personal soul contract I created for my soul to experience in this lifetime. What has it also done for me? This experience has reminded me of how courageous I am and very creative.

As I released my doubts and fears in my life, I discovered I am courageous and creative. This has brought me much happiness for myself.

Homework –

Think about your life and how it has flowed to this point. Start a time line of your life. While you write, this timeline put in it all events you remember. As you do this you will start to connect who your soulmates and soul group are.

Where have you planted the seeds of karma and what did you harvest from it?

What have you released?

I love you
I bless you
I thank you
I forgive you
I release you

I invite and invoke Arch Angel Michael to cut and cauterize all energetic cords leading in and out of me for my highest and greatest good. I invite and invoke Archeia Faith to fill me with Divine Light to heal all of my hurts and wounds. Thank you!

Spin a vortex –

Take a breath and quiet your mind.
Visualize a vortex or tornado circling your feet.
With each breath you take, the vortex rises over your body sinning faster and faster.

As the vortex spins you allow it to pull out of your field all those thoughts and energies that no longer serve you.

Visualize the vortex move up over your legs, hips, core, neck and head until you hear a pop. Your energetic field is now clear!

Notes:

Service

How often do you do something for someone else just for the wonderful feeling you get from the action?

How often do you feel inspired to do good for others? Do you follow through with your inspiration?

I often talk about keeping your heart open and aligned with the energy of love. When you can do that and keep that energy flowing through you it helps us with empathy, understanding and compassion. That way when we are inspired to help others, the action comes from our hearts, divine action.

What does the above have to do with service?

Those ideas are part of doing service for others. Just doing something nice for some because you can. Doesn't that give you the warm fuzzy feeling?

That is personal service. Then there is what I call 'community' service. This is when we do volunteer work, building houses, gardens, helping thrift stores. charities and more.

When you do this kind of work it is always wonderful to see the interactions of our community and the community comes together to work for a goal.

I always encourage people to do service, it is good for your heart and soul.

There is such a thing as karmic service too. Karmic service helps us balance out our karma in a big way.

I will give you an example of both personal and community karmic service.

I lived in Taos for about nine months. I knew I wouldn't live there for long when I landed in Taos and I knew I had some work to do as far as balance and growth.

Arriving in Taos I found myself volunteering for a place called the Shared Table at the Methodist church. There were three days when free lunches were served. We also put together donated items specifically for families with infants/toddlers to give out. I met some very interesting people there. I was balancing some community karma there. There were a couple of past lives where I wasn't a very nice person and this is how I decided to balance out my bad treatment of my community in the past by giving to the community in this lifetime.

I also met several people during this time, younger people. These people were runaways, abused and misled youths. I assisted them with getting to the next step in life or getting them safely back home. Balancing karma with them as well.

We also cleared two graveyards while we were there. Raising the resonance of Taos and bringing it into better harmony. Community service with the Earth.

While doing this work, I didn't think I was balancing karma. I was doing what I was inspired to do. Following through without being paid back or feeling as though I should be paid for the services. As I look back at these events I see that by doing these services I was released from being in Taos, I really don't like New Mexico, so as soon as my service was up new doors opened and I was able to move. I very gratefully left Taos and moved onto my next adventure.

I did feel like many burdens were released from my shoulders as I did my service in Taos, so by the time I left I did feel lighter and brighter.

Do you have times during your life where you were guided to serve others or do something nice for someone, just because? How did it make you feel?

I always encourage everyone if you are inspired, help out where you can. Be kind and follow your heart, you never know what will happen and it might give back to you in many wondrous ways.

Homework –

Random Acts of Kindness are a good wat to assist others in a heartfelt way. When you feel such a desire come to you, try it! Follow through from your heart and see how wondrous it is!

Do you feel inspired to help within your community? Follow through with your inspiration, you never know what it might lead too.

Have you ever done a deed and felt relief and release from doing it?

I invite and invoke Arch Angel Michael to cut and cauterize all energetic cords leading in and out of me for my highest and greatest good. I invite and invoke Archeia Faith to fill me with Divine Light to heal all of my hurts and wounds. Thank you!

Spin a vortex –

Take a breath and quiet your mind.
Visualize a vortex or tornado circling your feet.
With each breath you take, the vortex rises over your body sinning faster and faster.

As the vortex spins you allow it to pull out of your field all those thoughts and energies that no longer serve you.

Visualize the vortex move up over your legs, hips, core, neck and head until you hear a pop. Your energetic field is now clear!

Notes:

Timelines, Soul Contracts, Karma

I refer to timelines, especially when I do past life readings and soul retrieval. A Timeline is a breakdown of your life. Part of your homework is to write your timeline of your life.

Your Timeline is the map of your present and past lives. There is much to be learned about the self when working with your timeline. It shows you where you balanced karma and completed lessons or agreements you asked for before coming into this life. You may want to make different timelines for different parts of your life.

What is an agreement or contract?

Before we start each life time we map out what we want out of it. One of my agreements or contracts for this life is to create and enforce boundaries. I am often checking in with myself to make sure I am living my truth and ask myself, is this for my highest good? If it is not for my highest good, no matter how much it may hurt, I will let it go and move on. This is my life and I am living for my better good. Period.

Here is an example of a soul contract –

In 2009, I felt the need to move on from beautiful Colorado. My sons were at an age where they needed male guidance, a more stimulating environment. I asked their father to help. We decided to partner up again so he could assist with guiding our sons into adulthood.

I moved to Naperville, Illinois. I met a group of people, part of my soul group. I was able to balance out and resolve some karma, which helped me redefine the spiritual work I do.

Immediately in Illinois, I hit the ground running, or got busy finding a place to work out of, getting a regular job. One of the first places I visited to do readings was haunted, needed clearing, rearranging and assistance. I turned around before talking to anyone and walked out. I have a history of being a 'store closer.' If I worked in this place I would definitely need to help close this store down. I wanted a place I could work out of consistently for my stay in Illinois.

However, it didn't work out that way. I ended up working at that store, helping to clear it, clean it up and bring energy to it. Balancing Karma.

I met people there who I would work with during my time in Illinois. People I would learn to love, part of my soul group. Balancing Karma within the group.

Agreements and Karma do not have to be a struggle. If you are intelligent, creative and strategic you can balance Karma, settle soul contracts in a fun way.

I have an ongoing agreement of doing service for my community. I did my community service through A Gang of Girls Radio Show. The audience learned about new spiritual, metaphysical and paranormal ideas while my guests were able to reach the shows listeners. It was a very fun way of doing my community service. I love bringing the spiritual, metaphysical and paranormal community together.

When I stop to listen to my intuition and observe the souls who I am working with, I can tell when I am working on a karmic agreement or lesson. In balancing or understanding an agreement and completing what I set out to do for this lifetime assists everyone involved in the evolution of our souls.

Now when we make agreements we make them with many different kinds of souls. Your spirit guides, angels, ascended masters, cosmic beings are also learning as well while they are assisting us with our growth. WOW! Isn't that awesome? It is an equal exchange of energy. So, for those of you out there thinking you are burdening your spiritual team, you aren't, you are helping them. Lesson learned! Rock your life!

There are some people that really think they have to be 'special' in order to do spiritual/ healing work. Everyone is special, everyone carries the spark of the

Creator within them. 'Special' is ego. See everyone as being special and deserving, you certainly are.

I have heard people say, 'Hitler was a monster, how can he be special?'

Like all living beings on this planet, Hitler and those of his kind have a choice or many choices and are given the opportunity to choose a different path. Hitler taught us a lesson – how not to be. That's is a huge, global lesson to learn, evidently it was needed through all time and space. Not only did he teach people of his time how not to be, he taught further generations how not to be.

Look around our world, there is corruption everywhere, there is also Light and more people being present and making better choices. Make those choices that resonate with you. Put your energy into creating, manifesting your dreams whatever they may be. Ultimately it helps everyone connected to you and raises them up.

Homework –

What are your agreements with your spirit guides, angels, ascended masters or cosmic beings? How do you assist them and they assist you?

What are your agreements with your family?

Keep working on your timeline.

I invite and invoke Arch Angel Michael to cut and cauterize all energetic cords leading in and out of me for my highest and greatest good. I invite and invoke Archeia Faith to fill me with Divine Light to heal all of my hurts and wounds. Thank you!

Spin a vortex –

Take a breath and quiet your mind.
Visualize a vortex or tornado circling your feet.
With each breath you take, the vortex rises over your body sinning faster and faster.

As the vortex spins you allow it to pull out of your field all those thoughts and energies that no longer serve you.

Visualize the vortex move up over your legs, hips, core, neck and head until you hear a pop. Your energetic field is now clear!

Notes:

Clearing with Purpose

By the time, I was thirty-one years old, I was married, divorced, had my girl Jessica. After that I had a very passionate relationship with the father of my sons Xander and Risk. I was an emotional, heartbroken, angry wreck.

I left the father of my sons and Hawaii, I was heartbroken to leave both.

I left Oahu in February for Lynchburg, Virginia, where my Mom and Dad lived. I had two suites of luggage, car seat, a toddler, a little boy and four bucks in my pocket. Thank God for my parents and my brothers.

Have you been here in this situation? What did you do?

Well, I slept for a month pretty much. Then I woke up and hit the ground running. I knew I had to get it going on, I couldn't live with my parents for the rest of my life.

This is where I will be giving examples of soul contracts, karma, soul mates and getting clear, pay attention.

I started with selling jewelry. Back in the day it was different when you were a vendor. You actually had to go to the retail outlet, meet with the owner, manager or buyer to show your wares and sell or consign them. This is how I found my first spiritual teacher.

I walked into her art gallery and looked around. She looked directly into my eyes and said, "I have been waiting for you! Are you ready?"

I was surprised, intuitively I knew why I had been drawn to this art gallery. She was a great gift to me. She assisted me with clearing my heart and my mind during the eighteen months I lived in Virginia.

The first concept she gave to me was to clear the emotional baggage I inherited from my elders. One of the emotions I inherited was guilt. I was raised Roman Catholic, there is much guilt built into this belief system especially if you are a woman.

I always felt guilty, even as a child. The guilt came from the beliefs of my elders and the church. I was able to release the guilt as my first experience in clearing with purpose. This first experiment gave me the confidence to continue in this way of clearing. Every time I have a block I go back to these simple steps.

Remember using this way of clearing you can resolve many issues with your family members and assist those who are your clients. With this example I am going to write how I called forth my mother's spirit to release the guilt from the women directly related to me, my mother, grandmother, great grandmother and so on. With the emotional baggage cleared I was able to love these women without any if's ands or buts'. I had a better understanding of how they came to be the people they were and are in this moment.

My relationship with my own mother is awesome and we are able to relate so much better. She has changed her spiritual belief's over the past years and now meditates, listens to her intuition, has her own pendulum and ruin stones, she does readings for herself. This is a woman who fifteen years ago was afraid of tarot cards. Awesome ha?

Many families have certain beliefs or traditions that truly do not serve them. There are families that believe they are cursed. This way of clearing can clear this belief, past, present and future. It takes a lot of energy to create a curse, more than one person has to be involved with the creation of a true curse. If your family, ancestors spoke about a curse and continued to talk about the curse, they may have been the ones who created the curse by talking about it. Remember your words have power. Let's recreate that energy.

The most important concept of being an intuitive and or Medium is staying clear in mind, body and spirit. Keeping the self and energy field is very important.

Homework –
Work on Timelines

I invite and invoke Arch Angel Michael to cut and cauterize all energetic cords leading in and out of me for my highest and greatest good. I invite and invoke Archeia Faith to fill me with Divine Light to heal all of my hurts and wounds. Thank you!

Spin a vortex –

Take a breath and quiet your mind.
Visualize a vortex or tornado circling your feet.
With each breath you take, the vortex rises over your body sinning faster and faster.

As the vortex spins you allow it to pull out of your field all those thoughts and energies that no longer serve you.

Visualize the vortex move up over your legs, hips, core, neck and head until you hear a pop. Your energetic field is now clear!

Notes:

Spirit Guides

Before we start our clearing, we need to know who are our Spirit Guides.
Where do they come from?

Our Spirit Guides assist us throughout our life as a human on planet Earth. We have spirit guides that are with us from our first breath to our last breath. There are also what I call specialty spirit guides who come in to assist us with growth, projects, relationships etc.

Our Spirit guides can be our ancestors from this lifetime, our family members, friends who have passed through the veils. Our spirit guides can also be animals or pets who have passed on. We also have sprit guides who are people we have known in other lifetimes.

Spirit guides can be ascended masters, extraterrestrials, Galactic's, angelics, gods, goddesses, fairies, elementals and more. Remember this as you discover your spirit guides. I recommend reading Angels A Psychic's story to check out if any of the information there resonates with you.

If you are having dreams of pets, animals, family members or friends who have passed on, journal your dreams. Your spirit guides are giving you messages, messages to assist you on your soul's journey here on Earth.

In this day and age, we can research so many subjects. I know there is A LOT metaphysical information about animals. Look up the animal you have been dreaming, seeing or thinking about. What does this animal represent in your life?

Example – I have two wolves who are my spirit guides. One is black and the other is white. I picked them up at different times in my life and both are still with me.

When I started, my spiritual journey the black wolf came to me. This wolf helps me develop my discernment and temper my anger and frustration.

The White wolf came later on in my life. This wolf helps and inspires me with bringing unity within community.

When I lived in Pagosa Springs, I lived next door to the Wolf Refuge. I had never seen a wolf in person, let me just say this, they are huge. I used to watch the people walk those wolves down the dirt road we lived on.

I went to one of the fund raiser for the wolves, there were some of the wolves there at the fund raiser. I went in to make my donation and check out the art work. I was bumped in the back of my legs by a furry head. When I turned around, I saw the most beautiful, snow white, wolf. She sat down and looked up at me. Her trainer told me to be slow and careful. I put my hand out to the wolf and she put her head under it. Her fur was so soft and thick. I kneeled down next to her to look at her. She licked my face, now let me say this, wolves have big tongues. When she licked my face, she licked my whole face and rubbed her head on my face. I was so surprised by this and so was her nervous trainer. I was told to stand slowly and move away. I did stand slowly and that wolf drug her trainer after me through the gallery and outside. I watched as the trainer put the wolf back in her pen and retrieve another wolf. I sat next to the pen that held the white wolf for a while talking to her.

Has anything like that happen to you in this life?

Spirit guides nudge us along in our daily lives, illuminating or inspiring us to go or do a certain task. They help get us to the places we need to be to remember what we planned for our soul's journey. Don't dismiss those nudges, ideas, paths to your enlightenment. I always recommend having a small notebook with you to write down your inspirations, especially if you are very busy and don't have time to follow through with them in the moment. Look at them later and consider the ideas or inspirations.

When doing any kind of energy work or intuitive work it is always good to know who your spirit guides are. Not just know their names, but truly get to know them, what they feel, sound or look like or all of that. That way when you are being guided, you know who is guiding you. They are your best cheerleaders and best helpers.

I am very fond of St. Germaine, he has a very distinct energy that is quite lovely. I also just love Joseph of Arimathea. He is a most wondrous being, he was my uncle in his life time as Joseph of Arimathea. I am a trance channel for Mother Mary, Mary of Magdala, Lord Melchizedek and Lady Nada at the time of writing this book. They are all a great help while doing any kind of energy work, intuitive readings, soul retrieval, writing and speaking.

How do you know which wise spiritual master you work with?

I really resonated with the angels, so I researched them, I also worked with automatic writing meditations to help me. I have also researched Mother Mary and Mary of Magdala. I always felt the priests didn't have enough information about them. I started with the bible and then moved on to history books and other research material. I did this to get to know them.

I became aware of Lady Nada and the Pink Lightening

Angels in Colorado. Lady Nada and Archeia Grace have assisted me ease, grace and healing. When I do healing work, I can actually see Lady Nada guide my hands. When I realized who she was we had already built a good relationship through the healing work I was already doing.

It is good to know what each of your spirit guides feels like. This way you know who is advising and assisting you.

I do have a funny story about Lord Melchizedek.

When I lived in Virginia, I met a man I call Mr. Bill. He came looking for me, he calls me Mary. Why? He never explained it to me. Mr. Bill was already working with Lord Melchizedek on a pyramid project. He and I created some sacred tools during this time for his trip. Lord Melchizedek guided my hands while creating these projects and the prayer I said during their creation. I really resonated with Lord Melchizedek's energy during this time.

Another friend of mine, Chasteneka Eagle asked me to go with her to be ordained under the Order if Melchizedek. By this time, I was very curious about learning more about this wondrous being, I went with her.

I observed the ordainment of many people during this event. It was very intense. As I watched the priest give the ordainments, I saw all the karmic energy flying off the people as he was ordaining, I saw the energy in their energy fields clear and also what they would have to work on in their lives. I thought, wow, I am so not ready for this.

A couple of days later, Mr. Bill came to visit me. He asked me if I would like to be ordained under the Order of Melchizedek. He had no idea I had gone with Chasteneka. I told him no way, I was not interested in doing that. I had enough to do during that time. I described to him my experience at the ordainment. He advised me to go and have the ordainment because we both carry sacred items, having the ordainment would keep us out of trouble with having them. I told him, I would think about it, I also thought it would take a miracle to change my mind about getting ordained.

In Virginia, there was a week-long festival along the river, the bateau or flat boats raced the river from one point to the next each day. I decided to sell jewelry during this festival. On the third day of the festival I was setting up my stall in a meadow with very long grass. I noticed a man walk toward me with a white three-piece suit on. He was wearing a fancy white hat. I thought to myself, wow he must be hot, it was a hot day. The next thing I knew he was standing in front of me asking me if I knew anything about Lord Melchizedek, what?!

Honestly, I don't remember his exact words, during the conversation. The theme of the conversation was about Lord Melchizedek, how he is a great ascended master of the White Brotherhood and a great teacher. A group of Italian tourists came to my booth, I looked up and he was gone.

Was that a sign or what?

Mr. Bill asked me after I returned from the festival if I had changed my mind about the ordainment. I told him I would, I was curious and had experienced the man in the three-piece suit.

Have you had an experience like that?

Have you ever asked for guidance from your spirit guides and angels and been given a sign? If you have had experiences like that have you acted upon them? Did you act upon the signs given to you?

Your timelines will assist you with seeing signs your spirit guides were there with you communicating with you and giving you answers all along. What were the signs? How did they happen?

Homework –

It's time to discover your spirit guides!

Here is an easy way to start connecting with your spirit guides –
Stand in front of a mirror, turn the lights out and leave the door of the room open so you have a little light.
Look down toward your chin or up toward your eyebrows.

Ask to see, feel, hear, know your spirit guides for your highest and greatest good. – Very important!

Write down your experience. You may feel their presence first. Practice 3-5 minutes a day.

This method of seeing is called scrying. It is a very ancient way of seeing.

Work on Timelines

Automatic Writing Meditation – This will help you develop your relationship with your spirit guides through the written word and you will be able to connect what they feel like. The automatic writing meditation is on my website for you to use.

I invite and invoke Arch Angel Michael to cut and cauterize all energetic cords leading in and out of me for my highest and greatest good. I invite and invoke Archeia Faith to fill me with Divine Light to heal all of my hurts and wounds. Thank you!

Spin a vortex –

Take a breath and quiet your mind.
Visualize a vortex or tornado circling your feet.
With each breath you take, the vortex rises over your body sinning faster and faster.

As the vortex spins you allow it to pull out of your field all those thoughts and energies that no longer serve you.

Visualize the vortex move up over your legs, hips, core, neck and head until you hear a pop. Your energetic field is now clear!

Notes:

Sacred Space

Sacred Space is a space you create intentionally. What is it? It a place of safety, a safe place for yourself, family, friends or clients. My home is that, it is sacred space. I have it set up so when I work, I am always in a place where I am grounded, centered and connected. I endeavor to keep my place clean, clear and protected.

I wrote some of the ideas about protecting your home in I Am Psychic, not Telepathic, A Psychic's Story. This is where we go deeper and have more fun creating sacred space. This is where spirit guides, angels ascended masters, Galactic's and more come into place. In this chapter I will be referring to the Arch Angels, Archeia and guardian angels. For information about this group of celestials please read Angel's A Psychic's Story.

Your home is your sacred space. When you create sacred space, you will feel a true difference in your office or home. Sacred space allows whoever is in it feel safe and it also helps them clear or release, unwind and relax. As like when you clear your home, it may feel empty or clinical. That is ok, you are creating a pristine place to live or work in.

This is why it is always important to know who your spirit guides are and how they help you. Developing that relationship is truly important for any spiritual work you are doing.

Intention is a huge part of creating Sacred Space, why are you creating it? In this book, we will be creating Sacred Space for healing.

Before I create or enforce the space, I always say a prayer asking for the benefit of myself and or my clients highest and greatest good.

I always invite and invoke Archangel Michael and the Archeia Faith, first to guide, guard and protect everyone in my home, the people in it and my clients. Then I invite and invoke Arch Angel Uriel and Archeia Grace, for wisdom and guidance. Then the Arch Angel Gabriel and Archeia Hope for help with communication, they are also great with assisting children. Arch Angel Raphael and Archeia Joy for healing on all levels through all time and space.

I also work with several ascended masters. It also depends on what I am doing or working on. I will invoke Lady Nada and Lord Melchizedek. Why? They are my teachers. They assist with writing the Psychic's Story books, Clarity 101 blog and more. They are very inspiring and very wise.

When I start the invocations, I visualize a golden dome surrounding my office and forming underneath my feet.

Here is what it looks like –

1, Dear God and Goddess, please help myself and my client for our highest and greatest good through all space and time. Thank you!

2, I invite and invoke Archangel Michael, Archeia Faith, Arch Angel Gabriel, Archeia Hope, Arch Angel Uriel, Archeia Grace and Arch Angel Raphael and Archeia Joy to create sacred space for this healing through all time and space.

3, I invite Lord Melchizedek, Lady Nada and the Pink Lightening Angels to assist with this session.

You will feel your space shift into a place of safety and serenity.

When you are done –

4 I release you through all time and space with my greatest thanks.

I do this every day, in the morning for my sessions. Then I release after my last session.

Homework –

Create Sacred Space.

What spirit guides, angels, ascended masters, Galactic's are you working with?

Scrying 3-5minutes a day – journal what you are seeing, feeling or hearing.

Work on your Timeline

I invite and invoke Arch Angel Michael to cut and cauterize all energetic cords leading in and out of me for my highest and greatest good. I invite and invoke Archeia Faith to fill me with Divine Light to heal all of my hurts and wounds. Thank you!

Spin a vortex –

Take a breath and quiet your mind.
Visualize a vortex or tornado circling your feet.
With each breath you take, the vortex rises over your body sinning faster and faster.

As the vortex spins you allow it to pull out of your field all those thoughts and energies that no longer serve you.

Visualize the vortex move up over your legs, hips, core, neck and head until you hear a pop. Your energetic field is now clear!

Notes:

Clearing the Line

I don't know how many times I have been asked by my clients, is my family cursed?

First of all, it takes a lot of energy to curse someone. Most likely your family isn't cursed. It is a big project to curse someone. Most people don't want to take the time to do that anyway, repercussions of a curse are not fun. That's what I have to say about curses.

You might think your family is cursed because they have more 'bad luck' than 'good luck'. If seventy percent of your family think they are cursed, talk about being cursed, believe they are being cursed, this is a lot of energy being created into a curse. Many times, this is because there is no gratitude in the family. Start breaking the chain of creating a curse by being grateful. Thank you!

I was raised by my mother, grandmother and great grandmother. My great grandmother had lived through the great depression. We were poor growing up, yet I really did not realize it until I was older. My grandmother and great grandmother were very frustrated and often times angry people, very stubborn and set in their ways. They held all their grudges very close to them.

Their attitudes came from their parents and so on. Their attitudes infected the rest of the family and we carried a lot of them in our energy fields which did not help us. As I matured, I often wondered why I was such an angry person, guilty, unworthy and more.

I decided to research the religion I was brought up with, Catholicism. I ended up researching world history. Which taught me a lot about Christianity and how it evolved. It was a very empowering time for me and I had many realizations about how religion had influenced the women who raised me.

Religion, I believe has influenced many women about how they feel about themselves.

You are thinking, so what did you do about that Auriel?

It took me a while to think about how to 'Clear the Ancestral Line'. I truly believe the Archeia and Lord Melchizedek inspired me. I recommend you do this once a month. Focus on your father's or mother's line. You can alternate if you want too. You will start to feel lighter after about a week.

Progress takes times. It took my Mother's and my relationship several years to get to the place we are now, which is awesome!

Homework –

After doing this meditation, remember to journal how you feel. Continue to journal through the process.

Take a deep breath. Breathe in your favorite color and start to fill yourself with that color. Start with your toes. Keep filling your physical body with the color until you are full. When you can see, the color coming out the ends of your hair and pores of your skin, you are present and in your body.

Breathe deep and visualize a tornado or vortex around you. As you breathe allow the tornado to pull from you all those thoughts and emotions not serving you. Allow the tornado you clear your energy field. With each breath you take, feel the tornado move up your body to the top of your head and release the tornado out into the cosmos.

1, I invite and invoke Archeia Faith, Arch Angel Michael, Archeia Hope, Arch Angel Gabriel, Archeia Grace, Arch Angel Uriel, Archeia Joy, Arch Angel Raphael, Lord Melchizedek, Lady Nada and the Pink Lightening Angels to assist me, guide, guard and protect me during this session and afterward. (Invite those who you resonate with). Visualizing your golden dome.

2, Set your intention for the highest and greatest good for yourself and the parent you are working with.

3, Call forth the parent's name, their higher selves will join you in sacred space. When you feel, know, see their presence. Visualize a beautiful box, and place within it your, guilt, anger, frustration and whatever else you may feel that comes from your parents and or ancestors. Hand it back to your parent and let them know to fill the box and hand it back to their parent.

4, You will feel the energy moving from you and back up the Ancestral line.

5 Always thank your spirit guides, angels and ascended masters and release the energy of sacred space.

Repeat once a month until you feel you are clear of the energy binding you and your family.

Scrying 3-5minutes a day – journal what you are seeing, feeling or hearing.

Work on your Timeline

I invite and invoke Arch Angel Michael to cut and cauterize all energetic cords leading in and out of me for my highest and greatest good. I invite and invoke

Archeia Faith to fill me with Divine Light to heal all of my hurts and wounds. Thank you!

Spin a vortex –

Take a breath and quiet your mind.
Visualize a vortex or tornado circling your feet.
With each breath you take, the vortex rises over your body sinning faster and faster.

As the vortex spins you allow it to pull out of your field all those thoughts and energies that no longer serve you.

Visualize the vortex move up over your legs, hips, core, neck and head until you hear a pop. Your energetic field is now clear!

Notes:

Working with Others Energetically

When my youngest son was little he had a fear of me abandoning him. His fear was so deep he could feel me go into REM sleep and start crying, because he felt me shift onto the astral plane. He also suffered from really bad skin burning, and waking up exactly at one, every night crying. He was three years old. I was totally sleep deprived and needed to figure out what I could do to help both of us.

I asked my human teacher what I should do. She said, *'Call his higher self forth and find out what's going on with your son. His higher self can advise you on what you can do to ease and release. Figure it out, you can do it.'*

I asked my guides and angels, how to call his spirit forth to resolve these issues. The first issue I was guided was to help him release the abandonment issue.

I did call his higher self forth and asked about his abandonment issue. I was shown several lifetimes where I was the parent or guardian and he was abandoned. In these lifetimes, I was a roman soldier, who died in battle. Both my son and I died during the black plague, I died first. The last time I died after giving birth to him. I told my son's higher self I was sorry for those times that I left before him, it was not my intention. I let his higher self know, I was not going to abandon him. This life we came together to balance this energy out in this lifetime. By apologizing I balanced out the Soul Contract and released the energy of the abandonment issue.

After that, my son slept better. He stopped waking up as soon as I went into REM sleep. We were both happier people from being able to rest better.

I will note here, my son had a spirit friend/guide named Barney. Barney had to have a place at dinner, seat belt and so on. Yes, I could see Barney, he was a young soldier. He was one of my son's spirit guides and guards. He was very protective of my son. They did everything together. Risko, told me when he was almost four years old he wanted to be an army man when he grew up. He was not around anyone who was in the military and we did not talk about being in the army. We did not have television.

I took the next step to help his skin, he kept telling me his skin was burning, too hot. It looked like he had eczema. No matter how much oatmeal soap or baths he took, he still cried because his skin hurt him.

I called forth his higher self again to see what could be done for him. His higher self showed me a battle ground in Viet Nam. The image I was shown was of my son and Barney being blown up, that's why his skin was burning. His higher self told me there was residual energy around Risko of this particular lifetime. I called forth Barney and asked him to start talking to Risko about in this present lifetime he was safe, healthy and clear of his recent past life.

I started doing energy work on Risko to help release the layers of his Viet Nam lifetime. I also asked a friend of mine if she could make him some lotion or oils to help cool his skin. I also spoke to him about how he was safe and clear of his last life time.

It took some time before that lifetime was released. Working with his higher self all our guides and angels we were able to clear up his skin and waking up in the middle of the night.

I am writing this to let you know that you can help your children, spouse, friends etc. through this method. Which is similar to clearing your lineage. This method is deeper and it does take practice. Do not give up. Remember to journal each time you do this, so you can keep track of your successes. I have used this method for other people as well and have had success.

Children are always ready, they want to have fun and feel good. They may not understand their problems when they are awake This is why we do this work while they are asleep.

To do this kind of work you have to be present and in your body. You must practice discernment, be open and ready to receive messages in many different ways.

This is about healing, release and balance. Please use this way of healing with respect and love.

Homework –

Remember to journal what you see, feel, hear, know – your experience – the steps for balancing and clearing energy.

Take a deep breath. Breathe in your favorite color and start to fill yourself with that color. Start with your toes. Keep filling your physical body with the color until you are full. When you can see the color coming out the ends of your hair and pores of your skin, you are present and in your body.

Breathe deep and visualize a tornado around you. As you breathe allow the vortex/tornado to pull from you all those thoughts and emotions not serving you. Allow the vortex/tornado to clear your energy field. With each breath you take, feel the tornado move up your body to the top of your head and release the tornado out into the cosmos.

1, I invite and invoke Archeia Faith, Arch Angel Michael, Archeia Hope, Arch Angel Gabriel, Archeia Grace, Arch Angel Uriel, Archeia Joy, Arch Angel Raphael, Lord Melchizedek, Lady Nada and the Pink Lightening Angels to assist me, guide, guard and protect me during this session and afterward. (Invite those who you resonate with). Visualize your golden globe.

2, Set your intention for the highest and greatest good for yourself and the person you are working with.

3, Call forth the higher self of the person you are working with. You will feel the energy in sacred space shift as the higher self enters sacred space, you may see or hear the other person.

4, Ask – How can we resolve the issue for the highest and greatest good of everyone involved?

5, Be still and open to receive your information. If you have to write it down. If you have questions – ask them. This is your opportunity to heal or create balance.

6, When you are finished - Always thank your spirit guides, angels and ascended masters and release the energy of sacred space.

Remember to follow through with any instruction you receive.

Scrying 3-5minutes a day – journal what you are seeing, feeling or hearing.

Work on your Timeline

I invite and invoke Arch Angel Michael to cut and cauterize all energetic cords leading in and out of me for my highest and greatest good. I invite and invoke Archeia Faith to fill me with Divine Light to heal all of my hurts and wounds. Thank you!

Spin a vortex —

Take a breath and quiet your mind.
Visualize a vortex or tornado circling your feet.
With each breath you take, the vortex rises over your body sinning faster and faster.

As the vortex spins you allow it to pull out of your field all those thoughts and energies that no longer serve you.

Visualize the vortex move up over your legs, hips, core, neck and head until you hear a pop. Your energetic field is now clear!

Notes:

Earthbound Spirits & Travel Agents

Virginia is one of the most haunted places I have ever been too. Earthbound spirits are everywhere. I could look out the windows of the house I was living in and watch as the Civil War soldiers walked across the fields. It is very eerie.

I can see the Earthbound Spirits or ghosts. I can feel, hear and smell them. They don't really like being called ghosts. They are individual people who are usually stuck in a loop of their previous life, some are very intelligent and know what's going on, mostly they are waiting for something or someone.

When I was a little girl, spirits looked very much like real people. They were mostly nice to me and would warn me when something was going to happen or give advice. They were different from the angels, not scary, just different.

The Archeia and Arch Angel's look like real people too, when I am in their presence I feel loved, cherished and full of light. The Archeia and Arch Angels protected me from spirit attachments while I was a little girl and into my early thirties.

I did not have a spirit attachment until I lived in Virginia. The first spirit attachment I had was a former slave who had been beaten to death. First, I felt his pain, physical, mental and emotional pain. I had to force him to stand three feet outside of my energy field. I had to remind him several times as he was afraid I wouldn't assist him.

Once he was outside my energy field I was able to understand what he wanted. This spirit was waiting for his sweetheart. We opened a doorway for him to leave so he could find his sweetheart.

One of the ideas we have been taught is spirits are scary. They are only scary if you are scared of them. They do what they do to get attention. Most of the time, they just want to go 'home' or they are looking for someone.

When you are clear you know, or sense the discord around you. You want to be clear, grounded and centered, that way all messages you receive are clear.

These are the top three symptoms. If you feel this way clear your energy field –

Here are the symptoms of an attachment –
Dizzy
Nauseous
Have thoughts or feelings that you know aren't your own

Clear Your Energy Field

Take a deep breath. Breathe in your favorite color and start to fill yourself with that color. Start with your toes. Keep filling your physical body with the color until you are full. When you can see the color coming out the ends of your hair and pores of your skin, you are present and in your body.

Breathe deep and visualize a vortex/tornado around you. As you breathe allow the vortex/ tornado to pull from you all those thoughts and emotions not serving you. Allow the vortex/ tornado you clear your energy field. With each breath you take, feel the vortex/tornado move up your body to the top of your head and release the tornado out into the cosmos.

After you clear your energy field if you are still feeling off balance call a psychic medium to assist with the removal of the spirit attachment. Make sure it is someone you trust, read reviews and ask questions, get a referral.

I have had the opportunity to clear houses, people and objects. Clearing out spirits, sending them home, helps the environment, the people in the environment and raises the resonance of the person, place or thing.

Now when a spirit approaches me and asks to go 'home' or if I can help them find someone, I always help. I call myself a spirit travel agent. I don't stand around and talk to them, I just send them through. I am the person that opens the door for them so they can continue their souls journey.

For any kind of spirit that hurts you, makes your space smell bad, or if there are dead animals around call a trained and highly recommended paranormal team for assistance. If you can't find one let me know and I will refer one to you.

Travel Agent Checklist – Clearing Spirits from your energy Field –

Take a deep breath. Breathe in your favorite color and start to fill yourself with that color. Start with your toes. Keep filling your physical body with the color until you are full. When you can see the color coming out the ends of your hair and pores of your skin, you are present and in your body.

Breathe deep and visualize a vortex/tornado around you. As you breathe allow the vortex/tornado to pull from you all those thoughts and emotions not serving you. Allow the vortex/tornado you clear your energy field. With each breath you take, feel the vortex/tornado move up your body to the top of your head and release the tornado out into the cosmos.

Invite and invoke Arch Angel Michael and Archeia Faith to guide, guard and protect you.

I invite and invoke Arch Angel Michael and Archeia Faith, my guardian angel to guide, guard and protect me. I invite the Angels of Mercy Arch Angel Azrael and Archeia Serafina.

Remember to be firm, tell the being(s) to step three feet outside of your energy field so you can help. When this happens, visualize a window. Let the spirit know everything they want and desire is through the window. You will feel a shift in vibration when the being goes through the window. Close the window.

Spin a vortex again to clear your energy field.

When you are clear you will know, or sense any discord around you. You want to be clear, present and grounded so you can receive clear messages from yourself, guides, angels and ascended masters.

How do you know if it is messages from your higher self, guides, angels or ascended masters? You will feel cherished, loved, uplifted and wondrous.

Remember every time you work like this, work from your heart. Love and compassion can hear everything. This doesn't mean you are a push over. This means you are focused, direct and have set up some very firm boundaries.

If you feel you cannot do this on your own the first couple of times find a qualified practitioner to assist you.

Homework –

Is it part of your contract to be a travel agent/medium? How did you come to this conclusion?

Keep working on your timelines.

Scrying 3-5minutes a day – journal what you are seeing, feeling or hearing.

I invite and invoke Arch Angel Michael to cut and cauterize all energetic cords leading in and out of me for my highest and greatest good. I invite and invoke Archeia Faith to fill me with Divine Light to heal all of my hurts and wounds. Thank you!

Spin a vortex –

Take a breath and quiet your mind.
Visualize a vortex or tornado circling your feet.
With each breath you take, the vortex rises over your body sinning faster and faster.

As the vortex spins you allow it to pull out of your field all those thoughts and energies that no longer serve you.

Visualize the vortex move up over your legs, hips, core, neck and head until you hear a pop. Your energetic field is now clear!

Notes:

Haunted People

Fran and her mother walked into my bookstore one winter day. Fran had just been released from the psych ward. She was a mess on all levels, emotionally, mentally physically, spiritually. When I tuned into Fran, I saw the spirits attached to her and immediately called on Arch Angel Michael for her protection and mine. She cringed as soon as I invoked Arch Angel Michael, her spirit attachments had to move away from her.

Fran took a breath and said, "I am in need of your assistance. I can't do this on my own."

It took six months to help Fran get clear of her attachments. She went from a suicidal mess to a manager of a small motel during this time. How wondrous is that?

While working with Fran, I had the challenge if figuring out how to assist her in clearing the spirit attachments. I was guided to *'sort'* through her spirit guides and angels so I could clairvoyantly *'see'* and communicate with Fran's spirit attachments.

I sorted Fran twice a month for four months. We had to move out her spirit attachments in layers and work through some issues developed because of the spirit attachments. We started releasing the spirit attachments in stages. Starting from the most recent weakening the oldest spirit attached to Fran.

What happens when a person is haunted? They are drained of energy from the spirit attachments, are always being attacked or persuaded to do what the spirits want the human to do. This can cause emotional and mental breakdowns, leading to hospitalization and sometimes suicide.

I am giving you this example so you can understand the worst you might work with.

For most people, you may only have one or two layers to go through. I do not rush a clearing. I am very careful when clearing a person. With most clearings, your client might feel lonely and recall the spirits to fill the void. Warn your client this can happen. When they start to feel lonely they are to fill themselves with light and create an energetic egg around them with mirrors facing outward to keep their energetic field clear. Remind the client that are never alone, they are always surrounded by guides, angels and ascended masters.

Sorting

Take a deep breath. Breathe in your favorite color of the day and start to fill yourself with that color. Start with your toes. Keep filling your physical body with the color until you are full. When you can see the color coming out the ends of your hair, pores of your skin, you are present and in your body.

Breathe deep and visualize a tornado or vortex around you. As you breathe allow the vortex/tornado to pull from your energy field all those thoughts, emotions and energies that no longer serve you. Allow the tornado/vortex to clear you. You will feel the shift into clarity as this happens. When you feel this, release the tornado/ vortex and open your eyes.

Focus on your will or Solar Plexus and draw the energy up into your Heart and release the energy through your heart. This will assist with courage and love.

I invite and invoke Archeia Faith, Arch Angel Michael, Archeia Hope. Arch Angel Michael, Archeia Grace, Arch Angel Uriel, Archeia Charity and Arch Angel Jophiel. I invite and invoke Lord Melchizedek, Lady Nada and the Pink Lightening Angels, Arch Angel Azrael and Archeia Serafina to assist me, guide and protect me during this session and afterward. (In Place of these Angelics and ascended masters you may want to put your team in the invocation.) Visualize your golden globe.

Lead your client in breathing in their favorite color.

Look above your client with the intention of seeing, feeling, hearing or knowing where your client's guides are. When you make the connection -

Ask your clients Angels to move to their right side. Ask the Spirit Guides to move to the left side of your client. Ask the Ascended Masters to move to the center above your client's head. Ask the Fairies and elementals to move to the feet.

When you feel the shift, take a breath and look above the client again. You will see/feel/hear/know the attachments. Create a hallway with many doors and let the attached spirits know they are welcome to move through the doorway and down the hall to their door. Saying - *'Everything you want and desire in through the hallway'.*

You will feel/know/see/hear the shift as the spirit attachments leave through the hallway. When you feel/know/see/hear the client is clear of attachments spirit close the hallway door.

Release sacred space and say thank you for your assistance.

Homework –

Sort yourself.
Stand in front of a mirror, turn the lights out and leave the door of the room open so you have a little light.
Look down toward your chin or up toward your eyebrows.
Ask your angels to move to the right, Spirit Guides to the left, Ascended Masters and Cosmic Being above the head.
Fairies and Elementals by the feet
Ask everyone to move back three feet. Anything left in your energy field – hold a doorway open for them and let them know everything they want and desire is through the doorway.
When you are through – Spin a vortex.

What did it feel like? What did you realize about your spirit guides, angels, ascended master that assist you? Did you have some ah-ha moments of time when your spirit guides assisted you during your life?

Work on your timeline.

Scrying 3-5minutes a day – journal what you are seeing, feeling or hearing.

I invite and invoke Arch Angel Michael to cut and cauterize all energetic cords leading in and out of me for my highest and greatest good. I invite and invoke Archeia Faith to fill me with Divine Light to heal all of my hurts and wounds. Thank you!

Spin a vortex –

Take a breath and quiet your mind.
Visualize a vortex or tornado circling your feet.
With each breath you take, the vortex rises over your body sinning faster and faster.

As the vortex spins you allow it to pull out of your field all those thoughts and energies that no longer serve you.

Visualize the vortex move up over your legs, hips, core, neck and head until you hear a pop. Your energetic field is now clear!

Notes:

Clearing Haunted Places

On this planet, we have lots of different kinds of spirits. We have human spirit attachments, E.T.'s, Aliens, elemental or fairy and also we have darker hauntings.

Now I have experienced all of the above. I have met some wondrous spirits who have helped me and I have met some who I could truly do without.

In clearing these spaces, I always use salt and roses or the smell of roses. I do not burn sage. Most spirits don't like smoke. It can make the situation worse. I use kosher salt. Put it in glass bowls in the area where there is most activity. It absorbs sorrow, anger and frustration. Many spirits are sorrowful because they feel stuck for various earthly reasons.

So, if I am going into a dense place before I even start to clear the space I put salt down. If it is a house I put a circle around the house, salt the doorsteps and inside the house. Essential oils are good, rose oil is the best as it raises the resonance of the space or house. The smell of roses is the smell of unconditional love, unconditional love heals everything in all time and space.

Remember compassion is key with any clearing.

I always invite and invoke Arch Angel Michael and Archeia Faith, Arch Angel Azrael and Archeia Serafina to help guide guard and protect me through the clearing process.

'I invite and Invoke Arch Angel Michael and Archeia Faith to stand in this space to help raise the resonance of the place and to help release the spirits within this space. I invite and invoke, Arch Angel Azrael and Archeia Serafina *angels of mercy to help with the release of spirits in this place. I ask this for the highest and greatest good for all, so be it, so it is.'*

After the prayer, if the space is very dense, I wait three days. Then I go back to see if the spirits are ready to leave. Most of the time they are. I create a vortex that looks like a hallway with doors.

I encourage the spirits to walk through the doorway and let them know that everything they want and desire is on the on the other side of the doorway.

I encourage and send a lot of light. They need encouragement, compassion and light. Remember there is no bad or good, everything just is.

When the spirits leave, I feel the space shift, the resonance raises in the space. Close the vortex and put down more salt, use rose oil.

Release sacred space and say thank you.

When you are working on graveyards, battle grounds, jails, real icky places you may have to go back and do the release work with the spirits individually. There are many layers of density to work through in these places.

A bully is a spirit who holds other spirits back. You will have to work with them individually for the release of others. You have to convince them they are better off moving on than staying. Remember do this as compassionately as you can. If you go in thinking you are going to the bully you might find yourself in the middle of the mess. Be wise, straight forward and firm.

These types of places need as least three to twelve people.

I am going to give some examples here so you have something to relate too on your journey. Every time a space is cleared and spirits ascend, the place rises in resonance. When the place rises in resonance so does everything around it. So now you have assisted with the ascension of the spirits.

Intelligent Haunting – Excerpt from Haunted – A Psychic's Story

I lived in New Mexico for about 4 years. New Mexico is one of the strangest places I have experienced. The energy there is very strange. There are haunted places, aliens, UFO's and extra-terrestrial's. Not my favorite places to live or even visit.

My first experience in Taos was in a trailer I rented for the winter. I was grateful to get the trailer, it was close to a place where I was volunteering and centrally located to the different places I could work.

The trailer wasn't in the best shape when we moved in but we made it work. After about a week I started waking up in the middle of the night. At first I thought it was one of my kids waking up in the middle of the night. When I checked on them they were asleep.

I would look down the hallway to see if anyone was awake in my living room. I had three teenage girls sleeping in my living room. I asked the girls if they heard anything. One of the girls said she was woke up a couple of times from noises she heard.

We all started having experiences after two weeks in the trailer. We would look down the hallway and it would look like it was getting stretched out with a dark room at the end. The dark room was my bedroom. The bathroom started to become messy and no one liked to go in and if they did, no one wanted to close the door.

The spirit started scaring the kids. That's when I started to talk to it about leaving my sons alone. The spirit was not cooperative. I decided to take action with this spirit, obviously, it was pissed off at someone so I had to take action before this spirit got out of control.

I started putting kosher salt in little glass bowls around the house. Salt absorbs sorrow, anger and frustration. I waited a week. We were still feeling the energy, seeing the messes, but it seemed to calm down. I also told this spirit that we could live peacefully or it needed to leave. I invoked the Arch Angel Michael to protect the house and us.

I made salt lines in the doorways of my bedroom, bathroom and my sons room with the intention of keeping the spirit out of those rooms. Now it had the hallway kitchen and living room. It was the quiet before the storm.

My youngest son had to go to the bathroom in the middle of the night. I woke up to him crying in the hallway. I looked down the hall way and saw a darker being trying to connect with my son. The hallway was elongated and as I tried to get out of bed I felt like I was being held down. I got really angry and got up. I grabbed my son and growled. It left. I moved both of my sons in my bed for the night.

The next day I stood in the hallway and started talking to whatever it was that was haunting us. The spirit finally showed up. The spirit was a boy who had burned to death near the trailer. I didn't ask him about the event. I told him I could show him a better place to be. It took me a while to talk him into leaving the trailer. He finally left. The energy of the trailer changed drastically. I was so relieved to move into the trailer for the winter when we moved in I didn't realize how dingy it was.

After the spirit left and we sprayed the place down with rose spray to raise the vibration in the house and clear out the residual energy.

If you have anything like this happening on your property call a Paranormal Team. They will be able to assist you.

Another place we cleared in Taos was a large graveyard. The grave yard actually was not hard to clear. It took three of us to clear the yard. In this grave yard, there were E.T.s and spirits of animals and humans. This is one of my favorite clearings.

There was a guardian spirit of this graveyard. A Guardian spirit is a spirit who chose to assist with keeping an area clear or protecting spirits within their guardianship. I communicated with him three days prior to clearing. I let him know we were coming to release the spirits in the yard. He was very grateful and assisted us with the clearing.

I surrounded the yard with salt and recited my invocation.

When we arrived, the spirits were ready to go. I opened the great vortex for the spirits in the grave yard to leave.

Then I opened a vortex for the E.T.'s. We have to remember Alien's and E.T.'s do not come from this planet. Many times, their ships crash or they are left here. They perish and they also want to go home. They always go to a different place. At least this is what they tell me.

The clearing of this yard took three hours and we worked on it once.

Homework –

Have you been to a haunted location? Think about that place, what was it like? How did it make you feel? Did you see or intuitively know there were spirits in this house? With what you know now would you have cleared the place?

Work on your timeline.

Scrying 3-5minutes a day – journal what you are seeing, feeling or hearing.

I invite and invoke Arch Angel Michael to cut and cauterize all energetic cords leading in and out of me for my highest and greatest good. I invite and invoke Archeia Faith to fill me with Divine Light to heal all of my hurts and wounds. Thank you!

Spin a vortex –

Take a breath and quiet your mind.
Visualize a vortex or tornado circling your feet.
With each breath you take, the vortex rises over your body sinning faster and faster.

As the vortex spins you allow it to pull out of your field all those thoughts and energies that no longer serve you.

Visualize the vortex move up over your legs, hips, core, neck and head until you hear a pop. Your energetic field is now clear!

Notes:

Connecting the Dots

I am always asked, how I have been able to maintain my career as a professional psychic and soul retrieval practitioner, it is because I practice. I have met many intuitive people who were not professional psychic's, they practice every day. What I mean by practice is that what we do becomes habit and second nature, for example, spinning vortices and cutting cords every day. Reciting out intentions, creating sacred space, being present and aware of our environment. These are practices.

I love being 'clear', centered and balanced. I make better decisions. I can 'connect the dots' or connect to what is going on around me and utilize the information for my higher and better good and so can you. Practice, practice, practice! It will lighten your load and help you understand what your intentions and goals are for your soul's journey.

By flexing your intuitive muscles, you strengthen your intuitive skills and your connection to the Divine.

Practice what is in this book and the other A Psychic's Story Books. It will help you. My experiences have helped me considerably. I have balanced karma, completed agreements and cleared my families line for my children and grandchildren. I am grateful for the assistance. I hope you are too. Thank you!

Glossary of Terms

This is some of the vocabulary that is used and its respective meaning. This is written so that you the reader will have a reference and an understanding and some clarity of what is being discussed.

Akashic Records – In a location outside of time and space there is a library where everything is written down and accessible. If someone looks up your Akashic record, they are looking up all information about your soul, current, past and present.

Angel – Beings of Pure Light and Love who serve as messengers from our Divine Source

Ascension – A constant learning process through our lives as we come closer and closer to the Light. Every living being has the opportunity to Ascend!

Ascended Master – Spiritually enlightened beings who in past incarnations were ordinary humans, but who have undergone a process of spiritual transformation. The Ascended Masters have a great understanding of the human condition.

Aura – The energetic field that is the halo of light around a person, place or thing. The energetic field can be multicolored or one solid color, depending on the object or living being. The aura or energy field can fluctuate in color if the human being is ill or experiencing different emotions. An example is if a person is a smoker, the energy is usually closer to the body and there are black specks in it. If a person has cancer or some kind of chronic illness the spots are reflected in the aura.

Chakras – The seven energy centers of the body. Each Chakra has its own purpose and color and should be about two inches in diameter. The Chakra looks like a beautiful spinning vortex.

Channel – A trance channel is a person who fully incorporates an Ascended Master or Angelic.

Clairalience – Using your nose and your sense of smell, you can retrieve information. Some spirits have a certain scent that can be associated with them. Clairalience is the ability to detect these scents.

Clairaudience – To hear intuitively past our three-dimensional world clearly, hearing those who have passed over, Angels, guides, etc. Many of our mentally ill people are clairaudient and clairvoyant. It is not a linear way of being so their senses are dulled by medication prescribed to them by psychologists and medical doctors.

Claircognizance – 'Clear Knowing' as it is also knowing, is the ability to recognize and receive information from the ethers without dismissing it. Most Prophets are Claircognizant.

Clairgustance – 'You can literally taste it.' Clairgustance is the ability to taste information.

Clairsentience – 'Psychometry' is the ability to feel or touch objects or persons and receive knowledge about those objects or a person story.

Clairvoyance – The ability to see past our three-dimensional holographic world clearly. For example: Ghosts, Angels, Fairies, Spirit Guides, etc. As you work through the clarity classes you will develop sensitivity to seeing such things.

Disincarnate(s) – Ghosts. A human being who has died and their spirit are still on this earth plane. Many times, these spirits are still on Earth because they are lost or want resolution for the life they left.

Empathic – The ability to recognize and understand feelings of another person or persons.

Ether/Etheric or The Fifth Element – The place where Akashic information is stored is in the Etheric. It is all around us.

Fairy or Elemental – These are the teachers, guides and helpers of the earth. There are Fairies everywhere and are denoted by the four earth elements.

Sylphs – Fairies of air. Usually when you talk of Fairies, you think of sylphs.

Undines – Fairies of water.

Salamanders – Fairies of fire.

Gnomes – Fairies of earth.

Fairies range in all kinds of shapes and sizes. What is wondrous about Fairies is there is no hierarchy. All Fairies know their own importance and the importance of all other living beings.

Fwomp – Energy work either by fixing something, removing something, or adjusting something energetically.

Higher Self – The eternal core or essence of every living being.

Intuition – To take information from the ethers and interpret it in regards to self or others.

Invite – To give permission. It is a verbal allowance.

Invoke – To call for with earnest desire, pray for, and a way to bring in Archangels. When calling the angels, we both invite and invoke them.

Magic — To take something that is nonphysical and brings it into the physical.

Magician — A person who practices magic. All intuitive arts are performed by magicians who bring information from the ethers into the physical world.

About the Author

Auriel Grace is a practicing intuitive. Her specialty is being a Soul Retrieval Practitioner. During these sessions, she leads her clients into other lifetimes to assist with balance, release and clarity. For more information go to www.aurielgrace.net

Auriel has the ability to see into her other lifetimes and tell those stories.
The Book of Yzabelle & The Book of Ambyr are the first books in the Goddess Trilogy. These stories are lifetimes Auriel Grace has remembered and written!
Are you a part of those lifetimes?

Lucy Prophet is the first book of series of a young lady with a vision and how she 'sees' that through!
What would you do if you won the lottery?
Lucy Prophet Psychic Girl I
Lucy Prophet Psychic Girl II – 12/2016
Lucy Prophet Psychic Girl III 6/2018
Lucy Prophet & John Goode Honey Moon 6/2019

Evie Forest – Nature Girl – 2019
Evie & Ella – Children's Book - 2018

Are you interested in what to do about Hauntings? What are the different kinds? How can Angels Help you with a Haunting?
Haunted – A Psychic's Story 10/31/2016

What are Angels? How do they help us? How can we connect with them? Are they different from a Spirit Guide?
Angels – A Psychic's Story 12/2016
I am Psychic, Not Telepathic – A Psychic's Story 11/2017
Clearing with Purpose – A Psychic's Story 11/2018

Join Auriel Grace on Monday nights 8pm central when she hosts A Gang of Girls Radio on www.aurielgrace.net, leading you into new dimensions and metaphysical teachings.

Automatic Writing meditation and Ancestral Clearing Meditation is at – https://www.aurielgrace.net/meditations.html

Made in the USA
Middletown, DE
19 February 2019